Danny Kaye, Part 2 of 3

The Federal Bureau of Investigation (FBI)

The BiblioGov Project is an effort to expand awareness of the public documents and records of the U.S. Government via print publications. In broadening the public understanding of government and its work, an enlightened democracy can grow and prosper. Ranging from historic Congressional Bills to the most recent Budget of the United States Government, the BiblioGov Project spans a wealth of government information. These works are now made available through an environmentally friendly, print-on-demand basis, using only what is necessary to meet the required demands of an interested public. We invite you to learn of the records of the U.S. Government, heightening the knowledge and debate that can lead from such publications.

Included are the following Collections:

Budget of The United States Government
Presidential Documents
United States Code
Education Reports from ERIC
GAO Reports
History of Bills
House Rules and Manual
Public and Private Laws

Code of Federal Regulations
Congressional Documents
Economic Indicators
Federal Register
Government Manuals
House Journal
Privacy act Issuances
Statutes at Large

4-750 (Rev. 4-17-85)

XXXXXX
XXXXX
XXXXXX

FEDERAL BUREAU OF INVESTIGATION
FOIPA DELETED PAGE INFORMATION SHEET

_2_ Page(s) withheld entirely at this location in the file. One or more of the following statements, where indicated, explain this deletion.

☑ Deleted under exemption(s) _b7C and b7D_ with no segregable material available for release to you.

☐ Information pertained only to a third party with no reference to you or the subject of your request.

☐ Information pertained only to a third party. Your name is listed in the title only.

☐ Documents originated with another Government agency(ies). These documents were referred to that agency(ies) for review and direct response to you.

_____ Pages contain information furnished by another Government agency(ies). You will be advised by the FBI as to the releasability of this information following our consultation with the other agency(ies).

_____ Page(s) withheld for the following reason(s):

_____

_____

☐ For your information: _____

_____

☑ The following number is to be used for reference regarding these pages:

_65- 57412-227_
_-247_

XXXXXX
XXXXX
XXXXXX

XXXXXXXXXXXXXXXXXX
X   DELETED PAGE(S)   X
X NO DUPLICATION FEE X
X   FOR THIS PAGE   X
XXXXXXXXXXXXXXXXXX

FBI/DOJ

XXXXXX
XXXXXX
XXXXXX

FEDERAL BUREAU OF INVESTIGATION
FOIPA DELETED PAGE INFORMATION SHEET

___5___ Page(s) withheld entirely at this location in the file. One or more of the following statements, where indicated, explain this deletion.

☑ Deleted under exemption(s) ___b/___ with no segregable material available for release to you.

☐ Information pertained only to a third party with no reference to you or the subject of your request.

☐ Information pertained only to a third party. Your name is listed in the title only.

☐ Documents originated with another Government agency(ies). These documents were referred to that agency(ies) for review and direct response to you.

_____ Pages contain information furnished by another Government agency(ies). You will be advised by the FBI as to the releasability of this information following our consultation with the other agency(ies).

_____ Page(s) withheld for the following reason(s):

_____
_____

☐ For your information: _____
_____

☑ The following number is to be used for reference regarding these pages:
File numbers are classified. _____

XXXXXX
XXXXXX
XXXXXX

```
XXXXXXXXXXXXXXXXXXX
X  DELETED PAGE(S)  X
X NO DUPLICATION FEE X
X   FOR THIS PAGE    X
XXXXXXXXXXXXXXXXXXX
```

FBI/D

Office Memorandum • UNITED STATES GOVERNMENT

TO : MR. A. H. BELMONT

FROM : V. P. KEAY

SUBJECT: DANNY KAYE
INTERNAL SECURITY - C

DATE: October 8, 1951

Tolson
Ladd
Clegg
Glavin
Nichols
Rosen
Tracy
Harbo
Belmont
Mohr
Tele. Room
Nease
Gandy

████████████████ advised Mr. ████████████ in extreme confidence that the above-captioned individual had applied for a passport to go to Tokyo in connection with an entertainment tour. He stated that, in view of the existing derogatory subversive information regarding Kaye, his application for a military permit was turned down. He stated that Kaye's lawyer had approached the Department of the Army, and ████████████████ was called before the Secretary of the Army to state his reasons why Kaye should not be permitted to go to Tokyo. ████████████████ stated that Secretary Pace indicated that he would do whatever was suggested by ████████████████ ████████████████ further advised that ████████ ████████ brought pressure on certain individuals within the Department of the Army, and, as a result, Kaye was granted a military permit without ████████████████ being further consulted in the matter. ████████████████ was very much disturbed regarding this "undercutting" and "influence" being used by ████████████████

All b7C

████████████████ advised Mr. ████████████ in extreme confidence that he had communicated through a secret channel with ████████████████ advising ████████████████ of all of the facts and suggesting that Kaye be kept under a close 24-hours' surveillance the entire time he is in the Far East.

ACTION:

None.

ALL INFORMATION CONTAINED
HEREIN IS UNCLASSIFIED
DATE 12/2/88 BY SL-1MAU/813

This is submitted for your information. It should be noted that ████████████████ made this information available to Mr. ████████ in extreme confidence.

RECORDED - 19 ||/100 -
OCT 16 1951

SE 48

EX-141

384592

STANDARD FORM NO. 64

Office Memorandum • UNITED STATES GOVERNMENT

TO : Mr. A. H. Belmont   DATE: November 9, 1951

FROM : V. P. Keay

SUBJECT: DANNY KAYE

ALL INFORMATION CONTAINED
HEREIN IS UNCLASSIFIED
DATE 12/2/88 BY SP-7MRC/BS

Summary

PURPOSE:

To advise of name check requests received from the Office of the Secretary of Defense and from the Army-Military District of Washington, concerning Danny Kaye, motion picture actor. It has been ascertained that this inquiry has been made inasmuch as Kaye has offered his services to ███████████ as an entertainer and he is to be cleared for access to restricted areas.

INFORMATION IN BUREAU FILES:

A Selective Service Investigation was instituted concerning Danny Kaye on March 16, 1944, which was closed by report dated August 15, 1944. Allegations were received that Kaye simulated ████████████ conditions which caused him to be rejected at the induction station. After three days observation Army doctors advised that Kaye was █████████████ unfit for military duty. The U. S. Attorney for the Eastern District of New York declined prosecution.

A review of the Bureau's files reflect numerous references to Danny Kaye and these include information to the effect that in 194_ he was reported as being Treasurer of the Hollywood Section of the Independent Citizens Committee of the Arts, Sciences, and Professions and also in 1945 the official personnel of this organization were reported to be under Communist control.

The "New York Daily News" of April 27, 1951, reported that Danny Kaye was among those participating in a loyalty festival sponsored by a "Stop Communism Committee."

RECOMMENDATION:

INDEXED - 88
RECORDED - 88

100-384592 — 2

It is recommended that a copy of the Selective Service report and the attached memorandum be approved and returned to Supervisor ███████████ for transmittal to OSD and MDW-Army.

Attachment

DECLASSIFIED BY _____
ON _____

November 14, 1951

ALL INFORMATION CONTAINED
HEREIN IS UNCLASSIFIED
DATE 12/2/94 BY [initials]

DANNY KAYE
25-25177

There is being forwarded herewith a copy of an investigative report concerning the above-named individual, dated August 15, 1944.   (25-251771-2)

In 1945 it was reliably reported that Danny Kaye was Treasurer of the Hollywood Section of the Independent Citizens Committee of the Arts, Sciences, and Professions and his wife, Sylvia Fine, was an Executive Board member. Kaye has since been divorced from Sylvia Fine.   (100-338892-15X and 17)

In 1945 a campaign was being conducted against Gerald L. K. Smith by the County Headquarters of the Communist Party in Los Angeles County, California. A meeting for this purpose was held in which the National Association for the Advancement of Colored People; CIO; the National Center for Peace; the Americans United; and others participated. ████████████████ Danny Kaye was among those who

b7C   appeared. ████████████████
(100-254107-8)

b7D   ████████████████████████████████████
████████████████████████████████████
████████████████████████████████████
████████████████████████████████████
████████████████████████████████████
(100-344093-1)

It should be noted that the Independent Citizens Committee of the Arts, Sciences, and Professions had been cited as a Communist front by the Congressional Committee on Un-American Activities in a report dated April 19, 1949, and the California Committee on Un-American Activities report dated 1948, page 268.

Enclosure   b7C ████████████████

- Original to OSD

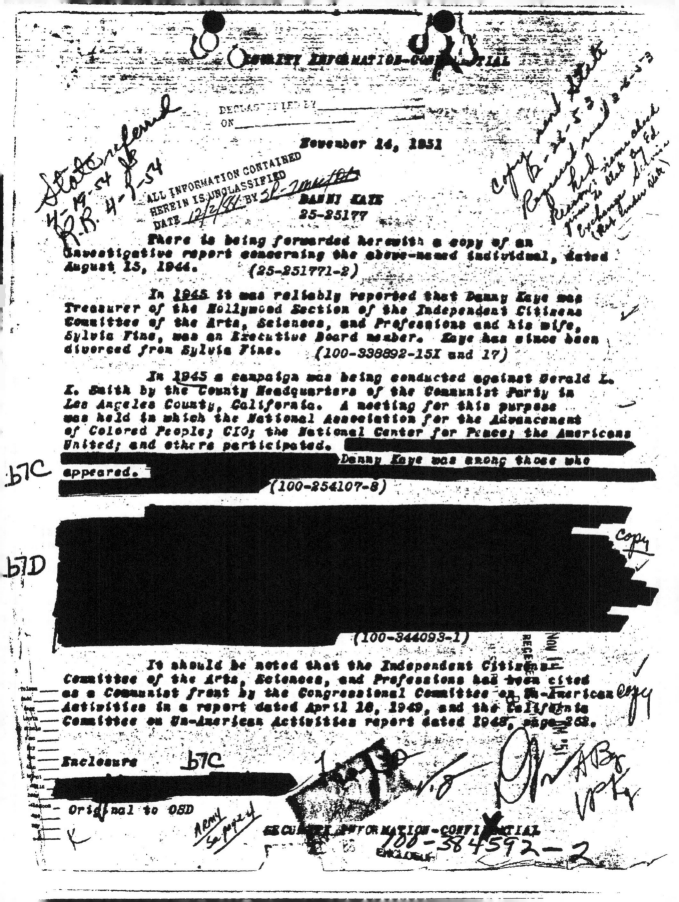

In September, 1945, a serious race disturbance developed at the Froebel High School in Gary, Indiana, caused by serious friction between the negro and white students at the school. In order to counteract the action of the white students in refusing to attend classes with the negroes, the Chicago Office of the American Youth for Democracy organized a special rally at Orchestra Hall in Chicago at which Danny Kaye appeared as the principal speaker. The rally took place on October 1, 1945, and all Chicago high school students were invited in order to prevent similar outbursts in Chicago schools.

b7D

The Chicago Action Council has been described by the "Sentinel", a weekly publication in Chicago, as a group "committed to the defeat and eradication of Fascism." (100-398935-3)

It should be noted that the American Youth for Democracy has been cited by the Attorney General as coming within the purview of Executive Order 9835.

The "Daily People's World" in its issue of September 26, 1945, carried an article reflecting that the fall semester of the Hollywood branch of the People's Educational Center opened on September 24, 1945, and that the emphasis of the teaching program would be upon peace and post-war problems and new cultural horizons. Particular publicity was given to the motion picture industry which had brought before the students film personalities, among whom was Danny Kaye. It is noted that the "Daily People's World" is a West Coast daily Communist publication and the People's Educational Center has been cited by the Attorney General as coming within the purview of Executive Order 9835.
(100-347118-18)

The "Washington Post" of October 27, 1947, contained a statement of the Committee for the First Amendment which protested "the continuing attempt of the House Committee on Un-American Activities to smear the motion picture industry." Among those signing this statement was Danny Kaye. (100-138754-Sub 1)

It is noted that the Committee for the First Amendment has been cited by the California Committee on Un-American Activities in its 1948 report, page 210, as follows: "A recently created Communist front in the defense of Communists and Communist fellow travelers. Its immediate purpose is to create favorable public opinion for the Communists who refused to testify before the House Committee on Un-American Activities in Washington, D. C."

The "Daily Worker" dated October 30, 1947, contained a news article concerning a "Stop Censorship" meeting which was to be held on October 30, 1947, at the International Theater,

Tolson
Ladd
Nichols
Belmont
Clegg
Glavin
Harbo
Rosen
Tracy
Laughlin
Tele. Rm.
Mohr
Sandy

- 8 -

Columbus Circle, New York City. The purpose of this meeting, according to the article, was to protest the "House Un-American" hearings which were being conducted in Washington, D. C. The article continued to state that at this meeting there would be a playback of the "Civil Liberties" broadcast made from Hollywood on the previous Sunday in which movie stars spoke on behalf of the witnesses who had been subpoenaed to testify before the House Committee on Un-American Activities. The article stated that this broadcast included Danny Kaye. (100-138754-A)

It has been reliably reported that on October 29, 1947, Danny Kaye, together with movie actors who had been in Washington, D. C., to support the Hollywood actors who refused to testify before the House Committee on Un-American Activities, stopped over in Philadelphia, Pennsylvania, en route back to Hollywood, and made a short radio broadcast commenting upon the Un-American Activities hearings in Washington. (100-138754-299)

The "Worker", a weekly Communist East Coast publication, on November 9, 1947, contained a news article concerning a radio show put on the previous Sunday by the Committee for the First Amendment, which broadcast protested the methods of the House Un-American Activities Committee. This article stated that Danny Kaye told of his trip to Washington with the 20 members of the Committee for the First Amendment. (100-138754-A)

According to the "Daily People's World", San Francisco, California, dated June 9, 1949, Danny Kaye was among those cited by the California Senate Committee on Un-American Activities as "typical of the individuals within the various Stalinist orbits about these activities and Stalinist programs and causes, this Committee has presented factual reports or has taken sworn evidence." (100-138754-A)

The "Daily Worker" of April 18, 1951, page 11, contained a column entitled "Why Are They Silent Today", which was written by David Platt. In this column Platt mentioned that during 1947 the Committee for the First Amendment was formed and representatives of the Committee went to Washington, D. C., where they presented a petition for "redress of grievances" to the Clerk of the House of Representatives in which it was charged that the investigative function of the House Committee on Un-American Activities had been "perverted from fair and impartial procedures to unfair, partial, and prejudiced methods." It was pointed out that numerous individuals signed this petition and among names listed was that of Danny Kaye. Platt in his article wanted to know why these people were silent at the present time.

SECURITY INFORMATION - CONFIDENTIAL

- 9 -

Copy

It is noted that in April, 1951, the House Committee on Un-American Activities was conducting additional hearings concerning Communism in the motion picture industry.

The "New York Daily News" of April 27, 1951, reported that on the preceding day a Stop Communism Committee was launched in order to fight against "Red influence in the entertainment world." This Committee was formed under the auspices of J. Joseph Smith, New York Commander of the Veterans of Foreign Wars, and the group was to hold a loyalty festival featuring more than 150 movie, stage, and television people, the day after the loyalty parade sponsored by the Veterans of Foreign Wars. The festival was to be held in Central Park and the stars scheduled to participate in the anti-Communist rally included Danny Kaye.   100-138754-835 page 58

Copy

The above information is furnished to you as a result of your request for an FBI file check only and is not to be construed as a clearance or nonclearance of the person involved. This information is furnished for your confidential use only and should not be disseminated outside your agency.

Enclosure

~~xxxxxxxxxxxxxxxxxxxxxxxx~~

cc-Assistant Chief of Staff, G-2
    Department of the Army
    The Pentagon
    Washington 25, D. C.

Tolson
Ladd
Nichols
Belmont
Clegg
Glavin
Harbo
Rosen
Tracy
Mohr
Tele. Rm.
Nease
Gandy

- 4 -

STANDARD FORM NO. 64

Office Memorandum • UNITED STATES GOVERNMENT

TO   : MR. A. H. BELMONT   DATE: May 6, 1952

FROM   : V. P. KEAY

SUBJECT: DANNY KAYE;
         ▮▮▮▮▮▮▮▮▮▮

         INFORMATION CONCERNING

     While discussing a film which is being produced about the Army, ▮▮▮▮▮▮▮▮▮▮▮▮ lapsed into a discussion of some of the problems he is faced with in clearing entertainers for the troops. Many of these entertainers who have left-wing backgrounds are trying hard to entertain the troops so that they could point to that achievement as indicative of their Americanism.

     He related that he had just recently refused permission to ▮▮▮▮▮▮▮▮ to entertain the troops. He also had refused permission to Danny Kaye on two occasions and had, however, been overruled by the higher echelons. He added that he would continue to refuse Danny Kaye every time his application came up, however, and leave it to the higher offices to clear him as he would never clear him. He has also refused permission to ▮▮▮▮▮▮▮▮▮ to entertain the troops.

ACTION:

     None. This is being submitted for your information.

All
b7C

ALL INFORMATION CONTAINED
HEREIN IS UNCLASSIFIED
DATE 12/2/88 BY SP-7/▮▮▮▮

RECORDED-30   100-384592-3

EX - 13 26   JUN 4 1952

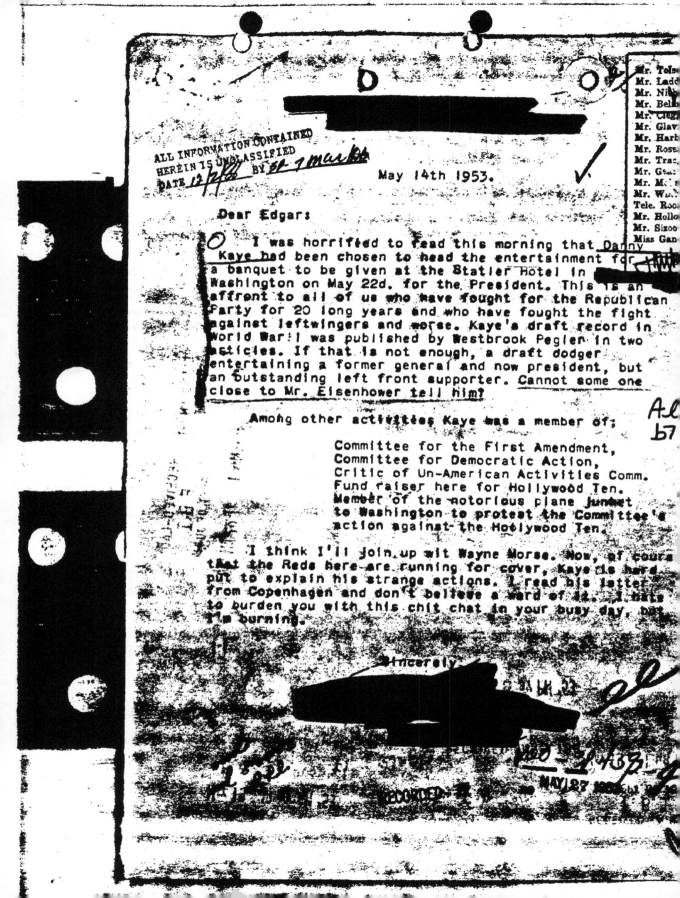

Mr. Tols____
Mr. Ladd
Mr. Nic____
Mr. Bel____
Mr. Cleg____
Mr. Glav____
Mr. Harb____
Mr. Rose____
Mr. Trac____
Mr. Gea____
Mr. M:____
Mr. Wu____
Tele. Roo____
Mr. Hollo____
Mr. Sizoo
Miss Gan____

May 14th 1953.

Dear Edgar:

I was horrified to read this morning that Danny Kaye had been chosen to head the entertainment for a banquet to be given at the Statler Hotel in Washington on May 22d. for the President. This is an affront to all of us who have fought for the Republican Party for 20 long years and who have fought the fight against leftwingers and worse. Kaye's draft record in World War!! was published by Westbrook Pegler in two articles. If that is not enough, a draft dodger entertaining a former general and now president, but an outstanding left front supporter. Cannot some one close to Mr. Eisenhower tell him?

Among other activities Kaye was a member of;

Committee for the First Amendment,
Committee for Democratic Action,
Critic of Un-American Activities Comm.
Fund raiser here for Hollywood Ten.
Member of the notorious plane junket
to Washington to protest the Committee's
action against the Hollywood Ten.

I think I'll join up wit Wayne Morse. Now, of course that the Reds here are running for cover, Kaye is hard put to explain his strange actions. I read his letter from Copenhagen and don't believe a word of it. I hate to burden you with this chit chat in your busy day, but I'm burning.

Sincerely

Al b7

b7

RECORDED   MAY 27 1953

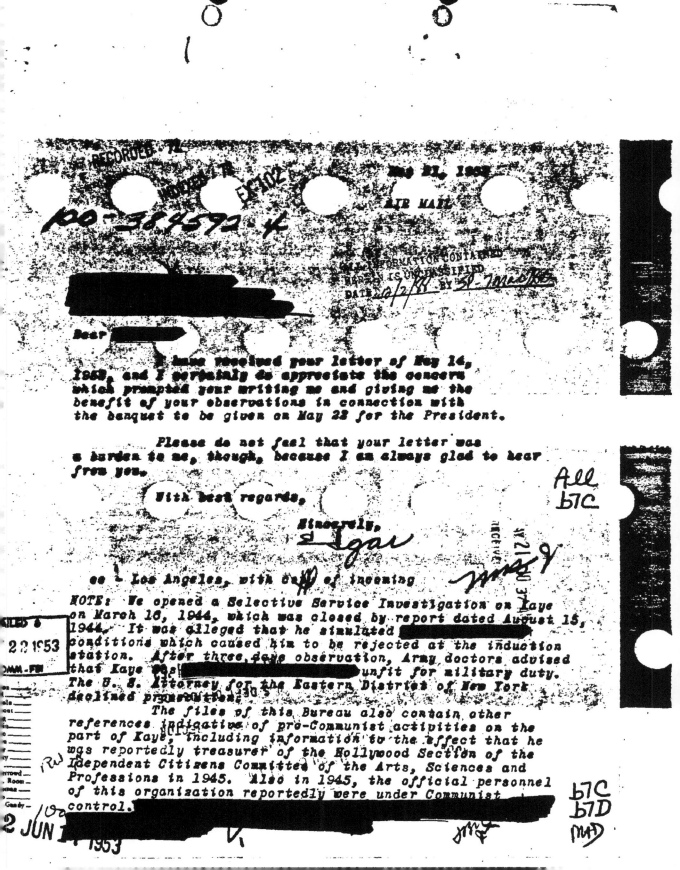

RECORDED 72
INDEXED 72   EX-102
100-384592-↓

May 21, 1953

AIR MAIL

ALL INFORMATION CONTAINED
HEREIN IS UNCLASSIFIED
DATE 10/2/XX BY SP-7MLC/RG

Dear ▮▮▮▮▮,

I have received your letter of May 14,
1953, and I certainly do appreciate the concern
which prompted your writing me and giving me the
benefit of your observations in connection with
the banquet to be given on May 22 for the President.

        Please do not feel that your letter was
a burden to me, though, because I am always glad to hear
from you.

        With best regards,

                Sincerely,

                E. Igar

All
b7C

cc — Los Angeles, with copy of incoming

NOTE: We opened a Selective Service Investigation on Kaye
on March 16, 1944, which was closed by report dated August 15,
1944. It was alleged that he simulated ▮▮▮▮▮▮▮▮▮▮
conditions which caused him to be rejected at the induction
station. After three days observation, Army doctors advised
that Kaye was ▮▮▮▮▮▮▮▮▮▮▮▮▮ unfit for military duty.
The U. S. Attorney for the Eastern District of New York
declined prosecution.

        The files of this Bureau also contain other
references indicative of pro-Communist activities on the
part of Kaye, including information to the effect that he
was reportedly treasurer of the Hollywood Section of the
Independent Citizens Committee of the Arts, Sciences and
Professions in 1945. Also in 1945, the official personnel
of this organization reportedly were under Communist
control.

b7C
b7D
MAD

FILED
2 2 1953
COMM-FBI

2 JUN 1953

4-750 (Rev. 4-17-85)

FEDERAL BUREAU OF INVESTIGATION
FOIPA DELETED PAGE INFORMATION SHEET

_/_ Page(s) withheld entirely at this location in the file. One or more of the following statements, where indicated, explain this deletion.

☑ Deleted under exemption(s) _b7D_ _____ with no segregable material available for release to you.

☐ Information pertained only to a third party with no reference to you or the subject of your request.

☐ Information pertained only to a third party. Your name is listed in the title only.

☐ Documents originated with another Government agency(ies). These documents were referred to that agency(ies) for review and direct response to you.

_____ Pages contain information furnished by another Government agency(ies). You will be advised by the FBI as to the releasability of this information following our consultation with the other agency(ies).

_____ Page(s) withheld for the following reason(s):

_____

_____

☐ For your information: _____

_____

☑ The following number is to be used for reference regarding these pages:
_100 - 384592 - 5_

FBI/DO

100 - 384599 - 5

RECORDED - 101

b7C

EX - 104

CLASSIFIED BY: *SP-7mce Pb*
DECLASSIFY ON: OADR *12/2/98*

Attention:

My dear

b1

(5)

The files of this Bureau reflect the following data concerning Kaye, also known as Daniel Kaye and David Kaminsky, which was his name before it was changed to Kaye.

b7D

It should be noted that the Independent Citizens Committee of the Arts, Sciences, and Professions has been cited as a Communist front by the Congressional Committee on Un-American Activities in a report dated April 18, 1949, and the California Committee on Un-American Activities report dated 1948.

Foreign Service Desk (Detached)

Tolson
Ladd
Nichols
Belmont
Clegg
Glavin
Harbo
Rosen
Tracy
Gearty
Mohr
Winterrowd
Tele. Room
Holloman

b7C

COMM - FBI
MAR - 1954
MAILED

In September, 1945, a serious race disturbance developed at the Froebel High School in Gary, Indiana, caused by serious friction between the Negro and white students at the school. In order to counteract the action of the white students in refusing to attend classes with the Negroes, the Chicago Office of the American Youth for Democracy organized a special rally at Orchestra Hall in Chicago at which Danny Kaye appeared as the principal speaker. The rally took place on October 1, 1945, and all Chicago high school students were invited in order to prevent similar outbursts in Chicago schools.

b7D

The Chicago Action Council has been described by the "Sentinel," a weekly published in Chicago, as a group "committed to the defeat and eradication of Fascism."

It should be noted that the American Youth for Democracy has been cited by the Attorney General of the United States as a Communist organization.

The "Daily People's World" in its issue of September 26, 1945, carried an article reflecting that the fall semester of the Hollywood branch of the People's Educational Center opened on September 24, 1945, and that the emphasis of the teaching program would be upon peace and post-war problems and new cultural horizons. Particular publicity was given to the motion picture industry which had brought before the students film personalities, among whom was Danny Kaye. It is noted that the "Daily People's World" is a west coast daily Communist publication and the People's Educational Center has been cited by the Attorney General of the United States as a Communist organization.

The "Washington Post" of October 27, 1947, contained a statement of the Committee for the First Amendment which protested "the continuing attempt of the House Committee on Un-American Activities to smear the motion picture industry." Among those signing this statement was Danny Kaye.

It is noted that the Committee for the First Amendment has been cited by the California Committee on Un-American Activities in its 1948 report as follows: "A recently created

Communist front in the defense of Communists and Communist
fellow travelers. Its immediate purpose is to create favorable
public opinion for the Communists who refused to testify before
the House Committee on Un-American Activities in Washington, D.C.

The "Daily Worker," an east coast Communist newspaper,
dated October 30, 1947, contained a news article concerning a
"Stop Censorship" meeting which was to be held on October 30,
1947, at the International Theater, Columbus Circle, New York,
New York. The purpose of this meeting, according to the article,
was to protest the "House Un-American" hearings which were being
conducted in Washington, D. C. The article continued to state
that at this meeting there would be a playback of the "Civil
Liberties" broadcast made from Hollywood, California, on the
previous Sunday in which movie stars spoke on behalf of the
witnesses who had been subpoenaed to testify before the House
Committee on Un-American Activities. The article stated that
this broadcast included Danny Kaye.

"The Worker," a weekly Communist east coast publication,
on November 9, 1947, contained a news article concerning a radio
show put on the previous Sunday by the Committee for the First
Amendment, which broadcast protested the methods of the House
Un-American Activities Committee. This article stated that
Danny Kaye told of his trip to Washington with the 26 members
of the Committee for the First Amendment.

According to the "Daily People's World," San Francisco,
California, dated June 9, 1949, Danny Kaye was among those cited
by the California Senate Committee on Un-American Activities as
"typical of the individuals within the various Stalinist orbits
about whose activities and Stalinist programs and causes, this
Committee has presented factual reports or has taken sworn
evidence."

The "Daily Worker" of April 13, 1951, contained a column
entitled "Why Are They Silent Today?," which was written by
David Platt. In this column Platt mentioned that during 1947 the
Committee for the First Amendment was formed and representatives

- 3 -

of the Committee went to Washington, D. C., where they presented a petition for "redress of grievances" to the Clerk of the House of Representatives in which it was charged that the investigative function of the House Committee on Un-American Activities had been "perverted from fair and impartial procedures to unfair, partial, and prejudiced methods." It was pointed out that numerous individuals signed this petition and among names listed was that of Danny Kaye. Platt in his article wanted to know why these people were silent at the present time.

It is noted that in April, 1951, the House Committee on Un-American Activities was conducting additional hearings concerning Communism in the motion picture industry.

The "New York Daily News" of April 27, 1951, reported that on the preceding day a Stop Communism Committee was launched in order to fight against "Red influence in the entertainment world." This Committee was formed under the auspices of J. Joseph Smith, New York Commander of the Veterans of Foreign Wars, and the group was to hold a loyalty festival featuring more than 150 movie, stage, and television people, the day after the loyalty parade sponsored by the Veterans of Foreign Wars. The festival was to be held in Central Park and the stars scheduled to participate in the anti-Communist rally included Danny Kaye. (100-384592-2)

The files of this Bureau also reflect that in 1943, Kaye was declared unfit for United States military service inasmuch as he was ▮▮▮▮▮▮▮▮▮▮ disqualified ▮▮▮▮▮▮▮▮▮▮ (25-251771)

b7C

The above data are being furnished you confidentially, should not be disseminated outside of your Organization, and should not be considered a clearance or a nonclearance by this Bureau of the individual involved.

Please be assured of my desire to cooperate in all matters of mutual interest.

Sincerely yours,

John Edgar Hoover
Director

- 4 -

MAILED
AUG 8 1955
NAME CHECK

August 8, 1955

DANNY KAYE
Born: January 18, 1913
Brooklyn, New York

CLASSIFIED BY: *58-71466/96*
DECLASSIFY ON: OADR 12/2/88

There is forwarded herewith a copy of an investigative report concerning the above-named individual dated August 15, 1944. (25-251771-2)

In addition to the above, FBI files reflect that an article published in the newspaper "PM" on July 15, 1945, quoted Sylvia Fine, wife of Danny Kaye, as stating that Danny Kaye was Treasurer of the Hollywood Section of the Independent Citizens Committee of the Arts, Sciences, and Professions and that Sylvia was an Executive Board member. (100-338892-17 p. 4)

The Independent Citizens Committee of the Arts, Sciences, and Professions has been cited as a Communist front by the Congressional Committee on Un-American Activities in a report dated April 18, 1949.

b7D

(100-344093-1) Source

Tolson _____
Boardman _____
Nichols _____ Enclosure
Belmont _____ Original and one to USIA
Harbo _____ Req. Rec'd: 7/18/55
Mohr _____
Parsons _____

b7C

RECORDED - 39 100-384592-6

In September, 1945, a serious race disturbance developed at the Proebel High School in Gary, Indiana, according to a confidential source who has furnished reliable information in the past, caused by serious friction between the negro and white students at the school. In order to counteract the action of the white students in refusing to attend classes, the Chicago Office of the American Youth for Democracy organized a special rally at Orchestra Hall in Chicago, at which Danny Kaye appeared as the principal speaker. The rally took place on October 1, 1945, and all Chicago High School students were invited in order to prevent similar outbursts in the Chicago schools.

b7D

The Chicago Action Council has been described by the "Sentinel," a weekly published in Chicago, as a group "committed to the defeat and eradication of Fascism."
(100-338935-3)   ) (C)

b1

It should be noted that the American Youth for Democracy has been cited by the Attorney General of the United States pursuant to Executive Order 10450.

The "Daily People's World" in the issue of September 26, 1945, carried an article reflecting that the Fall semester of the Hollywood Branch of the People's Educational Center opened on September 24, 1945, and that the emphasis of the teaching program would be upon peace and post-war problems and new cultural horizons. Particular publicity was given to the motion picture industry which had brought before the students film personalities, among whom was Danny Kaye. It is noted that the "Daily People's World" is a west coast daily Communist publication and the People's Educational Center has been designated by the Attorney General of the United States pursuant to Executive Order 10450.
(100-247118-18)

The "Washington Post" of October 27, 1947, contained a statement of the Committee for the First Amendment which protested "the continuing attempt of the House Committee on Un-American Activities to smear the motion picture industry." Among those signing this statement was Danny Kaye.
(100-138754 sub. A)

CONFIDENTIAL

The Committee for the First Amendment has been cited by the California Committee on Un-American Activities in its 1948 Report as follows: "A recently created Communist front in the defense of Communists and Communist fellow travelers. Its immediate purpose is to create favorable public opinion for the Communists who refused to testify before the House Committee on Un-American Activities in Washington, D. C."

The "Daily Worker" dated October 30, 1947, contained a news article concerning a "Stop Censorship" meeting which was to be held on October 30, 1947, at the International Theater, Columbus Circle, New York City. The purpose of this meeting, according to the article, was to protest the "House Un-American" hearings which were being conducted in Washington, D. C. The article continued to state that at this meeting there would be a playback of the "Civil Liberties" broadcast made from Hollywood on the previous Sunday in which movie stars spoke on behalf of the witnesses who had been subpoenaed to testify before the House Committee on Un-American Activities. The article stated that this broadcast included Danny Kaye. The "Daily Worker" is an east coast Communist newspaper.

The "Worker," a weekly Communist east coast (100-138754-Sub A) publication, on November 9, 1947, contained a news article concerning a radio show put on the previous Sunday by the Committee for the First Amendment, which broadcast protested the methods of the House Un-American Activities Committee. This article stated that Danny Kaye told of his trip to Washington with the 26 members of the Committee for the First Amendment.

(100-138754-Sub A)
According to the "Daily People's World," San Francisco, California, dated June 9, 1949, Danny Kaye was among those cited by the California Senate Committee on Un-American Activities as "typical of the individuals within the various Stalinist orbits about whose activities and Stalinist programs and causes, this Committee has presented factual reports or has taken sworn evidence."

- 3 -

CONFIDENTIAL

The "Daily Worker" of April 13, 1951, page 11, contained a column entitled "Why Are They Silent Today" which was written by David Platt. In this column Platt mentioned that during 1947 the Committee for the First Amendment was formed and the representatives of the Committee went to Washington, D. C., where they presented a petition for "Redress of Grievances" to the Clerk of the House of Representatives in which it was charged that the investigative function of the House Committee on Un-American Activities had been "perverted from fair and impartial procedures to unfair, partial, and prejudice methods." It was pointed out that numerous individuals signed this petition and among names listed was that of Danny Kaye. Platt in his article wanted to know why these people were silent at the present time.

It is noted that in April, 1951, the House Committee on Un-American Activities was conducting additional hearings concerning Communism in the motion picture industry.

The "New York Daily News" of April 27, 1951, reported that on the preceeding day a Stop Communism Committee was launched in order to fight against "Red Influence in the Entertainment World." This Committee was formed under the auspices of J. Joseph Smith, New York Commander of the Veterans of Foreign Wars, and the group was to hold a loyalty festival featuring more than 150 movie, stage, and television people, the day after the loyalty parade sponsored by the Veterans of Foreign Wars. The festival was to be held in Central Park and the stars scheduled to participate in the anti-Communist rally included Danny Kaye. (100-384592-2)

The foregoing information is furnished to you as the result of a request for an FBI file check and is not to be construed as a clearance or a nonclearance of the individual involved. This information is furnished for your use and should not be disseminated outside of your agency.

SEARCH SLIP

JUL 25 1955

Subj: *Kaye, Danny*

Supervisor _____   Room _____

R# *498* Date *7.17*   Searcher
                              Initial *9/0/*

	FILE NUMBER	SERIAL
SI.	25 - 251771	
I	100 - 384572 = 3-54	
I	100 - 384572-2 ...	
	11-9.5	
I	170 - 0 - 2425	
I	███████████████	
	Subj. VTD 1 ...	
	... 5-4-54	

b7C →

DO-6

OFFICE OF DIRECTOR
FEDERAL BUREAU OF INVESTIGATION
UNITED STATES DEPARTMENT OF JUSTICE

June 26, 1956

The secretary to Mr. Maxwell Rabb,
Cabinet Secretary called to confirm
the 3:00 PM today tour for comedian
DANNY KAYE, his wife and daughter.

Background memorandum is
attached.

They have requested to meet the
Director, and unless advised to the contrary they
will be announced to the Director upon their
arrival in the reception room.

Mr. Tolson
Mr. Nichols
Mr. Boardman
Mr. Belmont
Mr. Mason
Mr. Mohr
Mr. Parsons
Mr. Rosen
Mr. Tamm
Mr. Jones
Mr. Nease
Mr. Winterrowd
Tele. Room
Mr. Holloman
Miss Holmes
Miss Gandy

b7C

ALL INFORMATION CONTAINED
HEREIN IS UNCLASSIFIED
DATE 10/2/8 BY SP-2mas/88

ENCLOSURE

RECORDED - 79

INDEXED - 79

100-384592-7

JUN 27 1956

EX - 120

63 JUN 29 1956

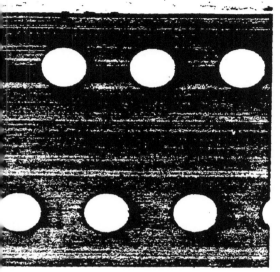

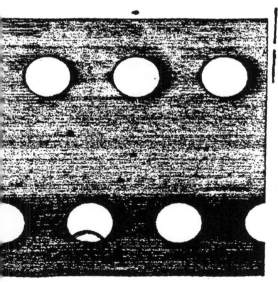

DO-6

OFFICE OF DIRECTOR
FEDERAL BUREAU OF INVESTIGATION
UNITED STATES DEPARTMENT OF JUSTICE

June 26, 1956

Mr. Tolson ✓
Mr. Nichols ✓
Mr. Boardman _____
Mr. Belmont _____
Mr. Mason _____
Mr. Mohr _____
Mr. Parsons _____
Mr. Rosen _____
Mr. Tamm _____
Mr. Nease ✓
Mr. Winterrowd _____
Tele. Room _____
Mr. Holloman _____
Miss Holmes _____
Miss Gandy _____

The Secretary to Mr. Maxwell Rabb, Cabinet Secretary, called in reference to the telephone call from Mr. Rabb yesterday concerning a tour for MR. DANNY KAYE. (Copy of call attached.)

The Secretary asked if we had contacted Mr. Kaye for a tour. After checking, she was advised that we had not contacted Mr. Kaye and that we were waiting for Mr. Kaye to call. The Secretary then stated that she would like to make tentative arrangements for MR. and MRS. KAYE to tour the Bureau this afternoon around 3:00 PM. The Secretary stated she would call later today to confirm the tour. Mr. Kaye has expressed a desire to meet the Director.

Arrangements have been made for an Agent from Crime Records Section to meet Mr. and Mrs. Kaye in the Director's Reception Room and conduct them on a very special tour of the Bureau, and unless advised to the contrary, they will be announced to the Director upon their arrival.

Background memorandum concerning Mr. Kaye is being prepared.

moe

Addendum: Based on a preliminary file check presently being conducted by the Crime Records Section, indications are that comedian Kaye was affiliated with several Communist Front Groups during the early 1940's.

b7C   continued

    File reflect that Kaye was also the subject
of a Selective Service violation case during the war
when it was alleged that he tried to simulate a ████████
████████ condition which would exempt him from
military duty. He was diagnosed by Doctors as
unfit for military duty.

Crime Records Section is presently preparing a
memorandum which will submitted to the Director
immediately upon its arrival in this office.

All
b7C

Office Memorandum · UNITED STATES GOVERNMENT

TO : Mr. Nichols

DATE: June 26, 1956

FROM : M. A. Jones

SUBJECT: DANNY KAYE
MEETING WITH DIRECTOR
6/26/56

ALL INFORMATION CONTAINED
HEREIN IS UNCLASSIFIED
DATE 12/2/88 BY SP-7mm/BB

Tolson _____
Nichols _____
Boardman _____
Belmont _____
Mason _____
Mohr _____
Parsons _____
Rosen _____
Tamm _____
Nease _____
Winterrowd _____
Tele. Room _____
Holloman _____
Gandy _____

PURPOSE:

To furnish brief account of information in Bufiles re Kaye, who, with his wife and daughter may see the Director at 3:00 P.M. today.

BIOGRAPHICAL DATA:

Danny Kaye - ~~~~~~~

Kaye is world-known actor and comedian who was born January 18, 1913, in New York City. His home and offices are in Beverly Hills, California. Most recent movies are "Knock on Wood" and "White Christmas," both in 1954.

BUREAU INVESTIGATION OF KAYE:

In 1944, allegation received that Kaye simulated a ████████████ condition causing rejection for military service. Kaye examined by army doctors who determined he was ██████████████ unfit for active military duty. Assistant United States Attorney declined prosecution. (25-251771)

MISCELLANEOUS:

Bufiles reflect Kaye's previous affiliation with communist activities in several communist front groups. ████████████████████ Also spoke at rally organized by American Youth For Democracy (cited by AG). He has been affiliated with Committee For the First Amendment which was critical of House Committee on Un-American Activities.

In 1949, Kaye, among several, described by California Un-American Activities Committee as "typical of the individuals within the various Stalinist orbits about whose activities and Stalinist programs and causes, this Committee has presented factual reports or has taken sworn evidence."

In May, 1953, ██████████████ in letter to Director, stated Kaye was member of Committee For the First Amendment, Committee For Democratic Action, fund raiser for Hollywood Ten and member of group who flew to Washington to protest HCUA action against the Hollywood Ten.

cc - Mr. Tolson
cc - Mr. Holloman

cc - Mr. Nichols
cc - Tour Room

100-384592-8

UNRECORDED COPY FILED IN

RECORDED
INDEXED

Memorandum to Mr. Nichols   June 26, 1956

    In 1951, Danny Kaye was participant in an anticommunist rally in New York City. ███████████████████████████████████

    Kaye was afforded tour of Bureau 11/20/40 but did not see the Director.

██

    Kaye and his All Star International Show are currently appearing at the Carter Barron Amphitheater in Rock Creek Park.

RECOMMENDATION:

    For information.

OFFICE OF DIRECTOR
FEDERAL BUREAU OF INVESTIGATION
UNITED STATES DEPARTMENT OF JUSTICE

4:03PM   June 25, 1956

Mr. Maxwell Rabb, Cabinet Secretary,
called to advise that he had talked to
MR. DANNY KAYE, the comedian,
and that he (Kaye) had expressed a
desire to bring his wife and son in
for a tour of the Bureau. Mr. Kaye
also expressed a desire to meet the
Director.

Mr. Rabb did not know just when Mr. Kaye wished
to take the tour, but wanted to alert us should Mr.
Kaye call this office.

Mr. Rabb said that should Mr. Kaye not contact
the Bureau, he thought it might be nice if we
were to contact Mr. Kaye at the Woodner Hotel
where he is staying.

Mr. Nichols has been advised.

Mr. Tolson
Mr. Nichols
Mr. Boardman
Mr. Belmont
Mr. Mason
Mr. Mohr
Mr. Parsons
Mr. Rosen
Mr. Tamm
Mr. Nease
Mr. Winterrowd
Tele. Room
Mr. Holloman
Miss Holmes
Miss Gandy

ALL INFORMATION CONTAINED
HEREIN IS UNCLASSIFIED
DATE 12/2/88 BY SP 7mac/883

b7C

100-384592-9

RECORDED - 64   JUN 29 1956

71 JUL 2 1956

Office Memorandum • UNITED STATES GOVERNMENT

TO : Mr. Nichols   DATE: June 26, 1956

FROM : M. A. Jones

ALL INFORMATION CONTAINED
HEREIN IS UNCLASSIFIED
DATE 12/2/88 BY SP-7muu/83

SUBJECT: SPECIAL TOUR
DANNY KAYE AND DAUGHTER, DENA Kaye

Tolson ✓
Nichols
Boardman
Belmont
Mason
Mohr
Parsons
Rosen
Tamm
Nease
Winterrowd
Tele. Room
Holloman
Gandy

Today at 3:00, Special Agent [redacted] met Kaye, his daughter and [redacted] in the Director's Reception Room to conduct them on a special tour. The tour had been arranged through Mr. Maxwell Rabb, White House. Rabb stated that Mrs. Kaye would accompany the group. Mrs. Kaye did not appear; however, [redacted] came along. There was a request to meet the Director and the Director spoke with this group.

All three individuals stated they were very thrilled on having the opportunity to see Mr. Hoover, and Mr. Kaye told his daughter that Mr. Hoover was one of the "greatest living Americans."

All b7c

The group then was conducted on a tour including visits to our exhibit rooms, the Laboratory and the range. Each one had the opportunity to fire the machine gun and was highly pleased with the results and requested the targets.

At the conclusion of the tour, each one personally thanked [redacted] for the courtesies extended and asked [redacted] to convey best regards to the Director.

The group was very congenial and seemed to enjoy the tour very much. Kaye asked [redacted] dozens of questions and appeared to be sincerely interested in our work.

RECOMMENDATION:

None. For information.

100-384592-10

INDEXED - 80

RECORDED - 8

z JUN 29 1956

cc - Mr. Holloman

[redacted]

(5)

TO : Mr. Nichols

DATE: July 3, 1956

FROM : M. A. Jones

SUBJECT: **MAXWELL M. RABB**
ARRANGEMENTS FOR SPECIAL TOUR

Tolson
Nichols
Boardman
Belmont
Mason
Mohr
Parsons
Rosen
Tamm
Nease
Winterrowd
Tele. Room
Holloman
Gandy

     Maxwell M. Rabb, who is the Cabinet Secretary at the White House, arranged a special tour for 10:30 this morning for his son, ▮▮▮▮▮▮▮▮ and the following individuals who are all in Washington with the Danny Kaye show which is playing here:

▮▮

     They were conducted on a special tour by SA ▮▮▮▮▮▮ ▮▮▮▮ Crime Records Section.

     The tour included the exhibit rooms, Laboratory and the range.

     There was no request to meet the Director. All were most enthusiastic about the tour and the work of the Bureau.

RECOMMENDATION:

     None. For information.

All
b7C

ALL INFORMATION CONTAINED
HEREIN IS UNCLASSIFIED
DATE 12/2/81 BY SP 7mau/BB

NOT RECORDED
146 JUL 9 1956

23 JUL 1956

CRIME REC.

JUL 12 1956

May 5, 1959

DANNY KAYE
Beverly Hills, California
DOB: January 18, 1913

Reference is made to your request that you
be furnished the results of any investigation conducted
concerning the captioned person, wherein information
of a subversive derogatory nature was developed. In
response to your request, you are referred to information
concerning Danny Kaye which was previously furnished
to the Department of State in February, 1953.
(100-384592-2)

Orig and one to State (SCA/ORM)
Req. rec'd 4/23/59

(4)   b7C

NOTE: State advised subject to be invited to White=
House Conference May 21-22. In view of very limited
backgound data furnished, State advised and concurred
that name check could be limited to "main security
file search " only.

ALL INFORMATION CONTAINED
HEREIN IS UNCLASSIFIED
DATE 12/2/88 BY SP-2mcc/fts

REC-39 100-384592-11

53 MAY 8 1959

25 MAY 6 1959

Tolson _____
Belmont _____
DeLoach _____
McGuire _____

Tele. _____

MAIL ROOM ☐   TELETYPE UNIT ☐

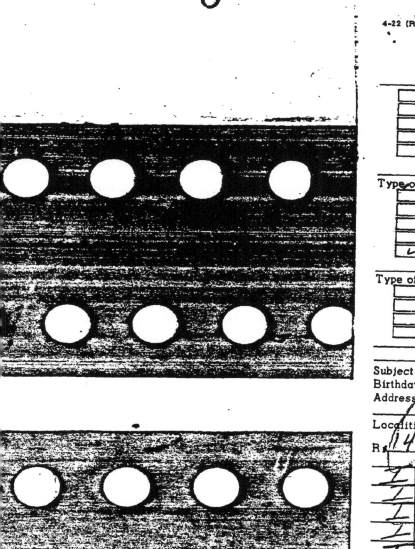

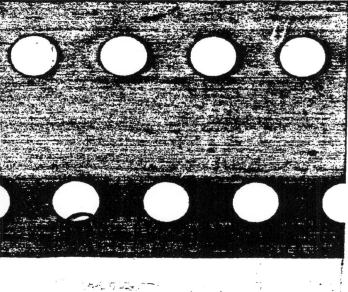

4-22 (Rev. 12-10-58)

Federal Bureau of Investigation
Records Branch

_____ , 195_

Type of References Requested:

☐ Regular Request (Analytical Search)
☐ All References (Subversive & Nonsubversive
☐ Subversive References Only
☐ Nonsubversive References Only
☑ Main ~~scalon~~ References Only

Type of Search Requested:

☐ Restricted to Locality of _____
☐ Exact Name Only (On the Nose)
☐ Buildup　　☐ Variations
☐ Check for Alphabetical Loyalty Form

Subject _Kaye Denny_

Birthdate & Place _____

Address _____

Localities _____

R _141_ Date _1/23_ Searcher Initials _S173_

	FILE NUMBER	SERIAL
I	25-251771	+
I	100-384592	
I	100-384592-2	Sum. 11-9-
I	-8 "	6 24-3
I	62-5-2295 Se. 7	" 113-7
	D.	

b7C _ℐ_ APR 27 1959

_ℐ_ ▓▓▓▓▓▓▓▓▓▓▓▓▓▓▓▓▓▓▓▓

FEDERAL BUREAU OF INVESTIGATION
FOIPA DELETED PAGE INFORMATION SHEET

_1_ Page(s) withheld entirely at this location in the file. One or more of the following statements, where indicated, explain this deletion.

☑ Deleted under exemption(s) ___b1___ with no segregable material available for release to you.

☐ Information pertained only to a third party with no reference to you or the subject of your request.

☐ Information pertained only to a third party. Your name is listed in the title only.

☐ Documents originated with another Government agency(ies). These documents were referred to that agency(ies) for review and direct response to you.

_____ Pages contain information furnished by another Government agency(ies). You will be advised by the FBI as to the releasability of this information following our consultation with the other agency(ies).

_____ Page(s) withheld for the following reason(s):

_____

_____

☐ For your information: _____

_____

☑ The following number is to be used for reference regarding these pages:
_100 - 384592 - 12_

FBI/DC

Bureau of Investigation
Washington,
D.C.
                    Danny Kaye
Gentlemen – I have been very
much disturbed at charges
of subversion made in public
about Danny Kaye and don't
know where to write to find
out the truth.

I am a member of the DAR
and an ardent GOP but I
am also a great believer
in the U.N. as an instrument
for keeping the

At a meeting of each of
these organizations.

EX-130   REG-19 100-384592-13

29 MAR 4 1960

Ack.
r Milwaukee
3-3-60

b7C

same person has made
charges of the infiltration
of Communism in the U.N.
and has openly used Danny
Kaye's name as being a spy
or subversive, implying
that your Bureau has proved
it.

If this is not true I should like
to have the facts to refute her
statements. I trust you can
send me such facts or tell
me where I can learn the truth.

Very truly yours

b7C

February 26-1960

HOTEL WAUSAU

Wausau, Wisconsin

Walter Schroeder, President   Telephone 4071

Bureau of Investigation
Washington,
D.C.

Gentlemen – I have been very much disturbed at charges of
subversion made in public about Danny Kaye and don't know
where to write to find out the truth.

I am a member of the DAR and an ardent GOP but I am also
a great believer in the U.N. as an instrument for keeping
the peace. At a meeting of each of these organizations,
the same person has made charges of the infiltration of
Communism in the U.N. and has openly used Danny Kaye's name
as being a spy or subversive, implying that your Bureau
has proved it.

If this is not true I should like to have the facts to
refute her statements. I trust you can send me such facts
or tell me where I can learn the truth.

Very truly yours,

/s/ ▓▓▓▓▓▓▓▓▓▓▓▓▓▓▓▓▓ b7C

February 26-1960

ALL INFORMATION CONTAINED
HEREIN IS UNCLASSIFIED
DATE 12/2/88 BY SP-7MC4/DB

March 3, 1960

EX-130

REC- 19

100-38459213

ALL INFORMATION CONTAINED
HEREIN IS UNCLASSIFIED
DATE 12/2/88 BY SP 1 mac/ea

██████████ aka, ████████████

Hotel Wausau
Wausau, Wisconsin

Dear ████████████

All
b7C

        Your letter dated February 26, 1960, has been
received, and the interest which prompted your communi-
cation is indeed appreciated.

        While I would like to be of assistance to you,
the function of the FBI as a fact-gathering agency does
not extend to furnishing evaluations or comments concerning the character or integrity of any individual,
publication or organization. I regret, therefore, that
I am unable to comply with your request for information
or advise where the information you desire may be
obtained.

                                Sincerely yours,

                                J. Edgar Hoover

                                John Edgar Hoover
                                Director

MAILED 19
MAR 3 - 1960
COMM-FBI

1 - Milwaukee (enclosure)

ATTENTION: SAC, MILWAUKEE

        Enclosed is a copy of correspondent's communi-
cation. Bufiles contain no identifiable data concerning
the correspondent.

NOTE TO MILWAUKEE, CONTINUED, PAGE TWO

SEE NOTE ON YELLOW, PAGE TWO

Tolson _____
Mohr _____
Parsons _____
Belmont _____
Callahan _____
DeLoach _____
Malone _____
McGuire _____
Rosen _____

Gandy _____   MAIL ROOM ☐ TELETYPE UNIT ☐

b7C

NOTE TO MILWAUKEE, CONTINUED

        Danny Kaye was the subject of a Selective Service
investigation in 1944 based upon receipt of an allegation
he had simulated a ███████████████ condition causing   b7C
rejection from military service. Kaye was later examined
by Army doctors who determined he was ███████████████
unfit for military duty. The United States Attorney
declined prosecution. Bufiles also reveal that Kaye was
associated with several communist front organizations in
1940; ██████████████████████████████
b7D ██████████████████████████ Kaye has not been the subject
of a Bureau security investigation. (100-384592)

NOTE ON YELLOW:

        Correspondent advises she has been disturbed
at "charges of subversion" made about Danny Kaye. Correspondent is a believer in the United Nations, but a
friend has made charges of communist infiltration into
the United Nations and named Kaye as a subversive or
spy. If this is not true, correspondent desires to have
the facts in order to refute these allegations.

- 2 -

DEPARTMENT OF STATE
WASHINGTON

March 28, 1961

FBI Liaison:	For Information Only
Re:	Danny Kaye. Born: January 28, 1911 Place: New York, New York
Residence:	1103 San Ysidro Drive Beverly Hills, California
Bureau File Number:	Unknown
Passport Number:	2505454 issued December 28, 1960 at Los Angeles
Attorney:	None

Travel Plans:

Port of Departure:	Unknown
Date of Departure:	December 31, 1960
Means of Transportation:	Unknown
Proposed Length of Stay:	Two months
Countries to be Visited:	England, France, Israel and Japan
Purpose of Trip:	UNICEF

NOT RECORDED
19 APR 24 1961

Copy to
by routing slip for
☐ info ☐ action
date
by

PASSPORT OFFICE
PT/L - Robert D. Johnson

Mr. Tolson
Mr. Belmont ✓
Mr. Mohr
Mr. Callahan
Mr. Conrad
Mr. DeLoach ✓
Mr. Evans
Mr. Malone
Mr. Rosen
Mr. Sullivan ✓
Mr. Tavel
Mr. Trotter
Tele. Room
Mr. Ingram
Miss Gandy

CARL HAYDEN, ARIZ., CHAIRMAN

RICHARD B. RUSSELL, GA.
DENNIS CHAVEZ, N. MEX.
ALLEN J. ELLENDER, LA.
LISTER HILL, ALA.
JOHN L. MC CLELLAN, ARK.
A. WILLIS ROBERTSON, VA.
WARREN G. MAGNUSON, WASH.
SPESSARD L. HOLLAND, FLA.
JOHN STENNIS, MISS.
JOHN O. PASTORE, R.I.
ESTES KEFAUVER, TENN.
A. S. MIKE MONRONEY, OKLA.
ALAN BIBLE, NEV.
ROBERT C. BYRD, W. VA.
GALE W. MC GEE, WYO.
HUBERT H. HUMPHREY, MINN.

STYLES BRIDGES, N.H.
LEVERETT SALTONSTALL, MASS.
MILTON R. YOUNG, N. DAK.
KARL E. MUNDT, S. DAK.
MARGARET CHASE SMITH, MAINE
HENRY DWORSHAK, IDAHO
THOMAS H. KUCHEL, CALIF.
ROMAN L. HRUSKA, NEBR.
GORDON ALLOTT, COLO.
ANDREW F. SCHOEPPEL, KANS.

EVERARD H. SMITH, CLERK
THOMAS J. SCOTT, ASST. CLERK

United States Senate
COMMITTEE ON APPROPRIATIONS

August 9, 1961

Honorable J. Edgar Hoover
Director, Federal Bureau of Investigation
Department of Justice
Washington 25, D. C.

Dear Mr. Hoover:

A few residents of my state have accused Danny Kaye, the well known Hollywood entertainer, of being a member of the Communist Party.

I would appreciate having your opinion whether there is any evidence to substantiate this charge. I might add that the basis of this charge seems to be derived from a tract entitled "The Reds are Back in Hollywood!!!" which is published by the Cinema Educational Guild, Inc., of Hollywood, California.

I should appreciate also any information you have as to the general accuracy of this tract and the reliability of this organization.

With kindest regards,

Sincerely yours,

THOMAS H. KUCHEL
United States Senator

REC- 68 100-384592 -14

9 AUG 31 1961

K:Ho

CORRESPONDENCE

EXP. PROC.

UNITED STATES GOVERNMENT

Memorandum

TO : Mr. DeLoach

FROM : M. A. Jones

DATE: 8-17-61

CLASSIFIED BY: SP-7mcc/88
DECLASSIFY ON: OADR 12/2/88

Tolson
Belmont
Mohr
Callahan
Conrad
DeLoach ✓
Evans
Malone
Rosen
Sullivan ✓
Tavel
Trotter
Tele. Room
Ingram
Gandy

SUBJECT: **INQUIRY FROM
SENATOR THOMAS H. KUCHEL
REGARDING DANNY KAYE** aka,
David Kaminsky

By letter dated 8-9-61 Senator Kuchel (R-California) noted that a few residents of his State had accused Danny Kaye, the well-known Hollywood entertainer, of being a member of the Communist Party. He requested the Director's opinion whether there is any evidence to substantiate this charge and in addition, noted that the basis of these charges against Kaye apparently derived from a tract entitled "The Reds Are Back in Hollywood!!!" which is published by the Cinema Educational Guild, Inc., of Hollywood, California. Senator Kuchel also requested any information concerning the general accuracy of this tract and the reliability of the organization.

INFORMATION IN BUREAU FILES:

We have enjoyed cordial correspondence with Senator Kuchel over the years, and he has been a member of the Senate since 11-2-54 when he was appointed to succeed former Vice President Richard M. Nixon.

Danny Kaye was born on 1-18-13 in New York City as David Kaminsky however, he changed his name to Danny Kaye. He was the subject of a Selective Service investigation in 1944 when it was alleged that he had simulated ██████████████ condition causing his rejection for military service. Kaye was later examined by Army doctors who determined he was ████████████ unfit for military duty, and the U.S. Attorney declined prosecution in the case. Bufiles also reveal that Kaye was associated with several communist front organizations in the 1940s; ████████████████████████████████████

Bureau security investigation; however, ██████████ Kaye has not been the subject of any ████

The ICCASP has been cited by the House Committee on Un-American Activities as a communist front.
Enclosure
1 - Mr. DeLoach

(3)

See next page...

Jones to DeLoach Memo
Re: SENATOR THOMAS H. KUCHEL

b7D

It was also reported in 1945 that Danny Kaye was the principal speaker at a rally held in Chicago by the American Youth for Democracy organization. The purpose of the rally was to prevent further racial disturbances in Chicago schools. ▓▓▓▓▓▓▓▓▓▓▓▓▓▓▓▓▓▓▓▓▓▓▓▓▓▓▓▓▓▓▓ It is noted that the Chicago Action Council has been described by the "Sentinel," a weekly newspaper published in Chicago, as a group "committed to the defeat and eradication of Fascism." In addition, the American Youth for Democracy has been cited pursuant to Executive Order 10450.

Danny Kaye has toured the Bureau on two occasions, the latter being with his wife and daughter on 6-26-56. During this latter tour he briefly shook hands with the Director.

b1

▓▓▓

(5)

(100-384592)

Other information of a public source nature regarding Danny Kaye has been prepared in the form of a blind memorandum and is attached.

The Bureau has received numerous inquiries regarding the Cinema Educational Guild and its tract entitled "The Reds Are Back in Hollywood!!!" This tract urges citizens not to patronize "Reds" in the movie and television industry and lists a number of actors, writers and et cetera whom they label as "Reds and fellow-travelers," among whom is the name Danny Kaye. We have not conducted an investigation of the Cinema Educational Guild; however, our discreet inquiries reflect it is allegedly an anticommunist group which has been responsible for the distribution of anticommunist, anti-Negro and anti-Semitic

b7C pamphlets. ▓▓▓▓▓▓▓▓▓▓▓▓▓▓▓▓▓▓▓▓▓▓▓ has in the past attempted to use the Director's name in furtherance of his programs and it has been necessary on several occasions to contact him and admonish him to refrain from mentioning the FBI in any manner.

RECOMMENDATION:

That someone in your (Mr. DeLoach's) Office contact Senator Kuchel regarding his inquiry and, if deemed appropriate, furnish him the attached blind memorandum containing public source information on Danny Kaye.

Suggest be handled verbally and no memo given

Adm. ▓▓▓ on 8/29/01

- 2 -

August 17, 1961

DANNY KAYE

An article in the newspaper "PM" on July 15, 1945, quoted Sylvia Fine, wife of Danny Kaye, as stating that her husband was treasurer of the Hollywood Section of the Independent Citizens Committee of the Arts, Sciences and Professions (ICCASP) and that Sylvia was an executive board member. The ICCASP has been cited by the House Committee on Un-American Activities (HCUA) as a communist front.

The "Daily People's World," in the issue of September 26, 1945, carried an article reflecting that the Fall semester of the Hollywood Branch of the People's Educational Center opened on September 24, 1945, and that the emphasis of the teaching program would be upon peace and postwar problems and new cultural horizons. Particular publicity was given to the motion picture industry which had brought before the students film personalities, among whom was Danny Kaye. It is noted that the "Daily People's World" was a west coast daily communist publication and the People's Educational Center has been designated by the Attorney General pursuant to Executive Order 10450.

"The Washington Post" of October 27, 1947, contained a statement of the Committee for the First Amendment (CFA) which protested "the continuing attempt of the House Committee on Un-American Activities to smear the motion picture industry." Among those signing this statement was Danny Kaye. The CFA has been cited by the California Committee on Un-American Activities in its 1948 Report as follows: "A recently created Communist front in the defense of Communists and Communist fellow travelers. Its immediate purpose is to create favorable public opinion for the Communists who refused to test before the House Committee on Un-American Activities in Washington, D. C

The "Daily Worker," dated October 30, 1947, contained a news article concerning a "Stop Censorship" meeting which was to be held on October 30, 1947, at the International Theater, Columbus Circle, New York City. The purpose of this meeting, according to the article, was to protest the "House Un-American" hearings which were being conducted in Washington, D. C. The article continued to state that at this

NOTE: See Jones to DeLoach memo captioned "Inquiry from Senator Thom Kuchel Regarding Danny Kaye," dated 8-17-61.

Tolson
Belmont
Mohr
Callahan
Conrad
DeLoach
Evans
Malone
Rosen
Sullivan

b7C

meeting there would be a playback of the "Civil Liberties" broadcast made from Hollywood on the previous Sunday in which movie stars spoke on behalf of the witnesses who had been subpoenaed to testify before the HCUA. The article stated that this broadcast included Danny Kaye. The "Daily Worker" was an east coast communist newspaper which suspended publication on January 13, 1958.

"The Worker," a weekly communist east coast publication, on November 9, 1947, contained a news article concerning a radio show put on the previous Sunday by the Committee for the First Amendment (CFA), which broadcast protested the methods of the HCUA. This article stated that Danny Kaye told of his trip to Washington with the 26 members of the CFA.

According to the "Daily People's World," San Francisco, California, dated June 9, 1949, Danny Kaye was among those cited by the California Senate Committee on Un-American Activities as "typical of the individuals within the various Stalinist orbits about whose activities and Stalinist programs and causes, this Committee has presented factual reports or has taken sworn evidence."

The "Daily Worker" of April 13, 1951, contained a column entitled "Why Are They Silent Today?" which was written by David Platt. In this column Platt mentioned that during 1947 the CFA was formed and the representatives of the Committee went to Washington, D. C., where they presented a petition for "Redress of Grievances" to the Clerk of the House of Representatives in which it was charged that the investigative function of the HCUA had been "perverted from fair and impartial procedures to unfair, partial, and prejudiced methods." It was pointed out that numerous individuals signed this petition and among names listed was that of Danny Kaye. Platt, in his article, wanted to know why these people were silent at the present time. It is noted that in April, 1951, the HCUA was conducting additional hearings concerning communism in the motion picture industry.

The "New York Daily News" of April 27, 1951, reported that on the preceding day a Stop Communism Committee was launched in order to fight against "Red Influence in the Entertainment World." This Committee was formed under the auspices of J. Joseph Smith, New York Commander of the Veterans of Foreign Wars, and the group was to hold a loyalty festival featuring more than 150 movie, stage and television people, the day after the loyalty parade sponsored by the Veterans of Foreign Wars. The festival was to be held in Central Park and the stars scheduled to participate in the anticommunist rally included Danny Kaye. (AE-5-2093)

DEPARTMENT OF STATE
WASHINGTON

IN REPLY REFER TO:

APR 21 1964

FBI LIAISON: FOR INFORMATION ONLY

RE: Danny Kaye
                              BORN: January 28, 1911
                              PLACE: New York, New York
                                      1103 San Ysidro Drive
RESIDENCE: Beverly Hills, California

BUREAU FILE NUMBER: Unknown

WASHINGTON FIELD OFFICE:

PASSPORT NUMBER: # 2505454 issued December 1960;
                                      Renewed March, 1964 at Los Angeles,
                                      California

ATTORNEY:

TRAVEL PLANS

PORT OF DEPARTURE: New York City

DATE OF DEPARTURE: June 15

MEANS OF TRANSPORTATION: Air

PROPOSED LENGTH OF STAY: Unknown

COUNTRIES TO BE VISITED: Europe

PURPOSE OF TRIP: Business   4

Copy to *Los Angeles*
by routing slip for
☑ info ☐ action
date 4-27-64
by _____

PASSPORT OFFICE
PT/L - ROBERT D. JOHNSON

Ingram Content Group UK Ltd.
Milton Keynes UK
UKHW030910120423
420037UK00008B/283